BarbwireDigi's
Guide to Creating
A Digital
Genealogy Scrapbook

Preserving your Family History Artistically

DATE

MONTH | DAY | YEAR

The 1880 Federal census shows
Fred Schwermann, a sailor, and his
wife Mary living at 626 Sixth Avenue
in Milwaukee, WI. They have four
daughters: Louisa (age 6) at school,
Emma (age 4), Alma (age 2) and
Antonetti (6 mo.).

MILWAUKEE, WIS.

1880
Schwerman
Family

BarbwireDigi's
Guide to Creating A Digital
Genealogy Scrapbook:

Preserving Your Family History Artistically

Barb Groth

BarbwireDigi

2014

ISBN 978-1-312-02923-1

Published by BarbwireDigi / Barb Groth
Barb Groth P.O. Box 687 PMB 147
Pinedale, Wyoming, 82941

BarbwireDigi.com

Ordering Information:

Special discounts are available on quantity purchases for genealogy associations, educators and others. For details, contact the publisher at the above listed address.

Dedication

This book is dedicated to those who endured the struggles, delighted in the daily challenges, celebrated the successes of life and made our present and futures possible

To My Family, Past and Present

Contents at a Glance

Contents

Acknowledgements

I wish to thank my husband, Jeff, who patiently stood by while I wrote this book and who was kind enough to review my draft page by page. Also thanks to my daughter, Carii, who bought me a gift certificate and got me started with digital scrapbooking only a few short years ago. Finally, a big thank you to my son, Eric, who accompanied me to Salt Lake City and back during a mammoth snow storm and stood by my side to help sell this book to many interested genealogists at RootsTech 2014..

Preface

A MESSAGE FROM THE AUTHOR

My hopes for this book are really quite simple. As a fellow genealogist, I know how many hours go into the search to find more about our families. Many of us have spent years visiting libraries, archives, repositories and days in front of a computer screen looking for just one more clue. One that might help us to understand more about those who proceeded us and shaped us into who we are today. I have a firm belief that all this laborious work and the many subsequent discoveries should not go unnoticed.

It has been said "a picture is worth a thousand words". That's really the beauty of scrapbooking ... it creates an end result that is interesting to view and can tell the story in such a way that it invites one to continue to turn the page and learn more. The other unique advantage is that by digitally creating the album, one is able to share it with others without having to be in their immediate proximity.

You have so much to offer. I do hope you'll make every attempt to use the guide and create your own unique, work-of-art about your family. Once you do, I sincerely hope that you will send a photo or a comment to my blog at: BarbwireDigi.com. Regardless, I thank you and I'm very certain your family will too!

Introduction

If you're anything like me, you embarked on this genealogy project without an inkling of where it might lead. But then, similar to what happens when you pick up a really good novel to read, you got "hooked". Although, unlike that mystery novel, genealogy research never seems to end. There's always one more piece of the puzzle that needs to be fit into place. That one *elusive* piece! So on you go – searching for more - and in the process, you discover more "loose ends".

And of course, in the process of uncovering your past, learning of those who proceeded you, supplied your genes, shaped your values, you begin to learn more about locations, history, events, time-lines, people, stories, facts, land records, faces, news, directories, probate, etc. than you ever dreamed possible. And while the note pages fill binders and the files fill drawers and you begin to really appreciate who you are and where you came from, two things are likely to occur:

> 1. You say to yourself "I really need to organize all this "stuff" I've collected. Just in case, by the remote chance, that someone might be interested in this vast collection of data; and

> 2. then, reality sets in – Will anyone really ever want to take the time, in this day and age of instant message, instant rice, audible downloaded books, to weed through these files, binders and books to see what I have found out?

I know when my kids read a book the first thing they do is look to the back to see how many pages they're going to "have" to read and if there are any photos or pictures to break up those dreaded pages of written word. So I fear that, although these findings of mine have been an interesting "project" and I've enjoyed the "journey", it may all end with me. Unless, of course, I am able to find a way to impart the knowledge in a more interesting way than my organized files, charts and binders.

Again, if you're anything like me, you're always working to undercover more but at the same time toying with the idea of what would be an informative, yet enjoyable format to present what you've found. Perhaps you've even been encouraged a little, as I was the day my daughter and I were driving through a neighborhood when I said, "Oh, this is where your dad's Aunt Pomplun lived ... they called her the Piccadilly Lady". To which she responded, "Mom, you know so much about these people, you should write it down." Really?! How exciting ... there is interest. Imagine that!

So I thought about writing a book. I even went so far as to buy a "how to" book as well as to outline how each surname might fit into the chapters and flow from one to another and note what the key events might be that would lure the reader into wanting to discover more about the "characters", my ancestors. Armed with the idea that a book was the way to go, I thought about creating an e-book so as to make the information more accessible to those, who like my daughter, I am no less than certain, will eventually want to learn all about our family. But visions of my children and their children counting the pages or looking at the total number of "locations" in an e-book before beginning the first chapter, made me hesitate to begin. Oh, and what if, heaven forbid, I find that elusive piece of the puzzle after the book is complete and then I need to rewrite the chapter, or the book for that matter. So my search continued to find the most interesting, workable means of presentation.

For years I put off writing even the first page. Procrastinating and assuming that I best wait until I had gathered more information. During this time, I renewed an old hobby, one that I enjoyed years ago when my daughter was competing in horseback riding events and my son was in wrestling - the hobby was scrapbooking. It was a great way to be creative and put all that memorabilia into something other than a shoe box or a file drawer. However, one thing about scrapbooking, there's a lot of material – photos, paper, embellishments, punches, adhesives, and more – If you move around a bit and aren't willing to tote the supplies with you, it's difficult to manage. So my hobby eventually evolved into digital scrapbooking.

I think you can see where this is headed. What a perfect combination - an interesting format which can combine not only photos but documents, journaling and other "scraps" into a "book" that can be not only informative but also interesting, even artistic. Once more, if you're anything like me, it's the perfect answer to the dilemma of how best to present and to share what you've gathered about your family's history and stories.

So what do you say, shall we get started? I'd love to show you how!

Chapter 1: Scrapbooks –

Yesterday and Today

Scrapbooks through the Ages

Scrapbooking has been around for ages as a means of preserving personal and family history. Typically, a scrapbook would contain photographs, printed media and other memorabilia.

Figure 1. Vintage Scrapbook

Although scrapbooking has evolved over the years, it is not all that different than in the 15th century, when collections known as *Commonplace Books* were created to include recipes, quotations, letters, poems and more. Later in the 16th century, *Friendship Albums* emerged which were the precursor to modern day yearbooks, containing friends names, titles and texts or illustrations. After the advent of modern photography in 1826, scrapbooks began to include this medium along with letters, newspaper clippings and other keepsakes.

Figure 2. Scrapbook Photograph Album

By the 1930's, scrapbooks emerged that were more like the photograph albums of today. You might be lucky enough to have one of these treasures (shown in Figure 3) and even more fortunate if the photographs were labeled with a name, location or date. [1]

Figure 3. Album of Family Photographs

Modern day scrapbooking is attributed to Marielen Christensen of Spanish Fork, Utah. She began designing creative pages of her family's mementos which she inserted into protective pages and collected in binders in the 1970's. By 1980, she displayed them at the World Conference on Records in Salt Lake City. [2]

The correlation between genealogy research presentations and scrapbooking is clear. After we've discovered more about our ancestors and our family tree in general, it's logical to display the information through the use of photos, letters, documents, etc. Scrapbooking certainly affords the means to do so.

However, as with anything, there are both advantages and disadvantages to this presentation format. The advantages include the fact that more than just the written word, as in a book, can be displayed; items such as cards, letters, maps, etc. can be incorporated into the page. The disadvantages of the classical form of scrapbooking, however, include the fact that the sizes of documents may not be ideal, the photos aren't necessarily cropped or enhanced and once the page is complete, it is very difficult to alter, if necessary. Furthermore, these pages and books are difficult to share and not very conducive to including the more recent types of records such as videos, recorded audio messages,

Digital Scrapbooks

While most "memory keepers", otherwise known as scrap bookers, prefer to use the traditional means of selecting papers and then building layer upon layer by pasting photos, quotes, embellishments, journaling and more on each; there are many who have converted totally or in part to a digital form of scrapbooking.

This newer method offers many benefits and conveniences, especially now that we're able to take advantage of the advances in scanning equipment, software, desktop publishing programs and the vast array of digital materials that are available, free or for purchase. Plus it is significantly easier to be a "mobile" scrap booker without having to lug reams of paper, cumbersome tools and accumulations of photos, embellishments and other paraphernalia. It can be more cost effective, since digital products, unlike papers, can be used multiple times without having to repurchase. One significant advantage, in my opinion, is the ability to resize, crop, enhance, clarify, edit and alter color in documents, photos and other materials.

Most genealogical data is already in a digital format so it stands to reason that a digital presentation format lends itself to this form of memory keeping and sharing. Plus, in itself, scrapbooking can be a very artistic and interesting arrangement of visual data.

Other compelling reasons to consider creating your genealogy research display in a digital scrapbook are its flexibility and ease of sharing. When you uncover additional facts, photos, relationships or other pieces of your family history, it's a relatively easy process to alter an existing page or book for that matter. And, because it's in a digital form, sharing can be easily accomplished by adding your work to an e-book, blog, email, web page, Microsoft® PowerPoint slide show, etc.

Additionally, the pages can be sent to any number of commercial photo book print companies in order to create a softcover or hardcover family photo album. Or, if you choose, print the individual pages commercially or on your own printer and insert them into your scrapbook binder.

Some scrap bookers use a combination of digital scrapbooking and traditional methods by printing the digital page and then adding additional embellishments to the page after it is printed, to give a three-dimensional look and feel to the pages. Pockets can be added for keepsakes and QR codes can be applied to provide a connection to videos, interviews or other audio/visual messages. The possibilities are endless!

Chapter 2: The Basics

Tools and Supplies

<u>EQUIPMENT</u>

There isn't really a lot in the way of equipment that is needed to get started in digital scrapbooking, but there are a few essentials and other "nice-to-haves". Here is the breakdown of what is needed in the way of hardware equipment.

1) Its fairly obvious that one of the most essential pieces of equipment you'll need is a computer. Your computer functions basically as your tabletop and the software replaces the tools and supplies typically used in traditional scrapbooking. Any brand will do but it's advantageous, since digital scrapbooking necessitates working with graphics, to have a faster model with a sizable screen monitor.

2) A scanner affords you the opportunity to go beyond merely including photos in your digital album. Consider scanning all sorts of memorabilia as well as older photographs, letters, brochures, maps, postcards, greeting cards, research documents such as census registrations, newspaper articles, obituaries, etc. I use an Epson® Scanner which can open wide enough to insert books or other larger pieces of memorabilia for scanning. Smaller, more portable, single page scanners like a ScanSnap® can be a convenient means of scanning and digitizing documents while offering the convenience of portability.

3) A digital camera is a useful piece of equipment but certainly not essential. This is especially true if your album does not deal with the present day. Photos can be obtained from anywhere and then scanned

into your computer in order to digitize them.

4) You may want to have an external hard drive or storage device. As you organize your photos, documents, digital elements and finished projects, you'll find that it takes quite a large portion of you internal hard drive storage. By storing some of the data on an external drive, you free up some of your computer memory. In addition, by using both an external hard drive and cloud-based storage, you will always have a means to back-up your digital works of art.

5) Finally, a printer is another useful, but not essential piece of equipment, especially if you choose to print your completed digital pages and assemble into a binder or an album. In many cases, however, since the pages are best created as 12" by 12", it is more cost effective to take your final product to a commercial printer or other entity to have them professionally printed. If you choose to use an 8" by 8" or 8.5" by 11.5" size, you will be able to print on your home/office printer however, you will lose the opportunity to read some of the print on documents, which must be smaller in size by necessity, in order to fit on the smaller page.

TUTORIALS

This e-book is designed to provide you with basic information so you'll know where to begin your project. However, keep in mind that there are over two million digital scrapbooking tutorials offered via the Internet that can guide you along the way. Many are free and very informative. Currently, Amazon sells over two thousand digital scrapbook guides and books, including *Digital Scrapbooking for Dummies*. Need I say more? Not only is digital scrapbooking popular but you'll find there is a lot of help available to you, if you're interested in learning more about the subject.

My personal preference is to enroll in one of the many classes that are available for purchase. These on-line class tutorials often offer free product(s), video demonstrations and PFD manuals for reference afterwards. A particular set of favorites are those offered by JessicaSprague.com or DigitalScrappers.com. By enrolling in their classes, one can learn not only the basic techniques but also the more advanced, as well as artistic, elements of digital scrapbooking. I'm also a fan of *The Daily Digi* (http://dailydigi.com) which offers everything from "Scrapbooking with your Computer Day One" to "Layout Design Tips" and "Techniques and Effects". There really is no end to the number of things an enthusiast can learn about the art of digital scrapbooking through on-line tutorials and classes.

You'll find that the software editing program you choose to use will provide their own set of tutorials as well. I currently use *Adobe Photoshop® Elements* software. Adobe has literally hundreds of movies on *Adobe TV* to guide you through everything from organizing and filing your media and documents, to adding special effects as well as sharing your digital creations. The sky is truly the limit when it comes to what you can learn and do with your photos and digital documents and it's growing daily!

DOWNLOAD FILES

An essential tool needed for digital scrapbooking is photo editing software. In order to facilitate the process, you'll need a digital software program such as *Adobe Photoshop®* or *Adobe Photoshop® Elements*, *Memory Mixer, FotoFusion, Hallmark Scrapbook Studio, Craft Artist Platinum Edition* or *My Memories Suite* – just to name a few. Their price ranges and capabilities vary greatly. *Adobe®* offers a free 30-day trial of these programs in its latest version.

My preferred program is *Adobe Photoshop® Elements* and it's the software that will be used in the demonstration of creating a genealogy scrapbook in this book. I also will be utilizing *Yin Design Templates*. It is not essential to use templates but these, in particular, offer great page designs and make the process so much easier than starting from scratch that they're well worth the investment.

You'll discover an incredible number of offerings available for purchase from many creative digital artists. These include digital kits, papers, fonts, brushes, embellishments, masks, overlays and much more – all of which can help to make for some awesome works of art. These items are by no means essential for the process but can be very useful. You may also find that many designers offer free items on their websites. There are literally hundreds to choose from but I have assembled a listing below of my personal favorites:

http://www.digitalscrapper.com/

http://thedailydigi.com/

http://www.designerdigitals.com/

http://www.jessicasprague.com/

http://www.digiscrapaddicts.com/

http://www.scrapbookgraphics.com/

Not only can you use these sites to purchase digital supplies and sign up for on-line classes, but they are also loaded with ideas and designs for the pages you'll be creating for your album. "Scraplifting" is a common practice among scrap bookers, both digital and traditional, and it is perfectly acceptable. "Scraplifting" means you are stealing, or should I say borrowing, scrapbook ideas from another person's layout as you create your own. Many digital designer sites have galleries where digital pages are posted. These are great inspirational tools to use when searching for ideas on what to make a page look like or just to get your creative juices flowing. I recommend putting a file folder on your computer, named "Design Ideas", and use it storing copies of the layouts you like once you've found them on-line.

Organize and Save

COMPUTER FILES

Since it's your own unique scrapbook, it will include a significant amount of your research information and data. Therefore, it is essential that the documents you may wish to include are organized in files where they can be easily accessed. These would include not only your family group sheets and charts, but also your sources such as census data, naturalization forms, military draft records, city directories, probate information, church records, land records, newspaper articles, letters and more. Nothing is more frustrating, while you're in the midst of scrapbooking, than knowing you have a photo or a map or a certificate that you want to include, but having no idea where you stored it.

You'll want to personalize your digital scrapbook as much as possible with family photos and stories. So it is vitally important that all of these pieces of information are organized ahead of time as well.

My recommendation is to order *Sassy Jane's Guide to Organizing Your Genealogical Research Using Archival Principals* at http://www.sassyjanegenealogy.com/. It's the best guide I have found yet for organizing everything on your computer that you might later need to find and use when you're ready to get to work on your digital scrap-book pages.

I might also suggest that before you begin to work on a scrapbook page, you copy all the items that you think you might want to include and place them in a file folder on your desktop. That way you'll have quick and easy access when you're ready to begin to create your digital scrapbook page and the process will be significantly more efficient. It's not to say you can't add an additional item that comes to mind while you're in the midst of creating the page, but it's a great, time-savings means of getting underway.

PHOTOS, STORIES AND INTERVIEWS

Since the goal is to have the genealogy scrapbook you're creating be of interest to others, it should contain photos along with copies of research documents. While documents may provide sources of information, it is far more interesting to look at photos and graphic design, as opposed to a page made up solely of written word and forms. Some of your pages may go back to an era where you don't have photographs of your ancestors. If you don't have photos of family members that are a part of the story you're attempting to relay, then you can incorporate interest with other images. Some suggestions include items such as maps, photos of cities or houses, postcards, vintage photos and pictures of other tokens or memorabilia. The combination of various photographs and other graphics does wonders to make the overall page more interesting and artistic. As was the case with your documents, you'll want to organize your photos and other graphic materials in a way so as to make them readily accessible and easily found.

Journaling is also a very important part of the digital scrapbook. After all, your stories are a crucial part of bringing together everything that you've uncovered about your family and making the presentation more than just a research paper. They truly individualize the scrapbook and make it your own. You may know what the research tells the observer about who, what, where, when, etc. but the real interest comes from the details and stories that perhaps only you know. So be sure to share what you can on each page. There are several ways to do this by writing anything from a short blurb to several paragraphs. Don't neglect to do so. It's likely to be the most important and interesting part of your creation.

Interviews can also be incorporated into the scrapbook since its digital. In this day and age of modern technology with tablets and phones that take videos, YouTube, Screencasts, and QR codes, there are a number of ways to make the recording or the video be a part of your album. You'll see how this can happen, when we go through the information in Chapter Six.

PLAN THE ALBUM

Finally, it's essential that you plan the general flow of the digital scrapbook album. You'll want to do so before you begin so that there is a logical approach to the presentation. There are many options:

- Present day and work backwards,

- Begin with the past and work forwards,

- Focus on one ancestor,

- Select one surname,

- Choose a family or,

- Include multiple families or

- Base it on significant events

Using the basic guide of who, what, where, when and how can be helpful. Also, keep in mind who your audience is and what you'd really like to have them know about what you've found.

You may choose to include a table of contents, a source page or an index like any other book. It may also be helpful to break your album into sections by generations. You may wish to use color coding or formatting to differentiate between an ancestor's family and or a generation. The most important thing is to have a plan beforehand for your scrapbook in general.

Individual pages can be planned according to what you have in the way of photos, documents, etc. as well as what you want to share. Building the page is somewhat similar to the traditional paper method where you build upon a page layer by layer. There is no right or wrong way to make your work of art, but in the end you'll find you have a masterpiece that will help you distribute your story in an artistic format that you'll be pleased to share with others. It's likely to live long after your files and records have gathered dust in an attic or storage space, perhaps for many generations to come! And the best part is that you personally made it. It's one of a kind

Chapter 3: Creating the Scrapbook

Adobe Photoshop® Elements

We begin with the commercial photo editing software that is the basis for working on the project. Although there are a number of photo editing software programs available in the marketplace, I prefer to use *Adobe Photoshop® Elements*. It may not be as inexpensive as other choices, but in my opinion, it offers the most options and support. The program not only allows you to organize and enhance your photos but also to create layouts, using multiple images, and to easily share your finished product via print, web and more. Free trials of the software are available and once you've had a chance to use the product, if you find the results to be favorable, you can then purchase it. Go to www.Adobe.com and select *Adobe Photoshop® Elements* products.

ORIENTATION TO ADOBE PHOTOSHOP

When you start *Adobe Photoshop® Elements*, you'll see that you have a choice of "Organizer" (left side) or "Photo Editor" (right side). As we design the Digital scrapbook, we will work primarily in "Photo Editor" mode, however you'll find that "Organizer" can be a convenient means to store photos so that they are readily accessible.

Figure 4. The Welcome Screen

After selecting "Photo Editor", there will be three options on the top portion of the screen – Quick, Guided and Expert. Quick offers a simple, expeditious fix for photo alterations and repair. The Guided option gives just that, a guided means of editing photos and adding special effects. For the purposes of digital scrapbooking, the Expert option is the one to choose. It supplies the means to not only edit but also to create digital designs.

Once the Expert option is selected, the desktop screen will appear. Several features of the desktop will be familiar. On top is the Menu Bar. It contains the following selections: file, edit, image, enhance, layer, select, filter, view, window and help. Each offers a drop-down list of numerous choices.

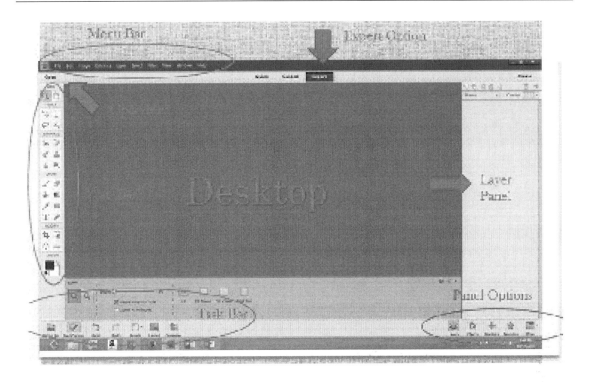

Figure 5. Adobe Photoshop® Elements Desktop

The Tool Bar is located on the left side of the desktop. Tools are grouped according to their main function – View, Select, Enhance, Draw, Modify and Color. More options are available for each tool by selecting "Tool Options" in the Task Bar.

You'll find the Task Bar at the bottom of the desktop. It contains shortcut icons, including Photo Bin, Tool Options, Undo, Redo, Rotate, Layout and Organizer.

On the right side of the Task Bar are Panels for Layers, Effects and several other options as noted under "Windows" in the Menu Bar. Most of our work is done in the Layers panel so a future section will go into greater detail on Layers.

PHOTOSHOP® ELEMENTS MENU

To begin your digital scrapbooking project, you can choose to start from scratch by selecting file, then pick "new" and "blank file" and then create the size page that you want.   A standard size is 12" x 12" however 8" x 8" is also popular.

In order to work with documents, photos and other items, they must first be brought from your computer files into the *Adobe Photoshop® Elements* program. There are several ways to move files:

•   Click on the word **OPEN** that appears below the Menu bar and above the Tool bar on the left side of the desktop,

•   Click "File" on the Menu bar, then select "Open", or

•   Use the keyboard shortcut by clicking on "Control" and on the letter "O".

Figure 6. The "OPEN" Option appears beneath the Menu Bar

The elements of your page will be in a number of different formats. Photos are typically in the JPEG or GIF format. While templates are in PSD (this is also the format your scrapbook page will be in until you save it as a JPEG – more on this later). Documents will be in either JPEG or TIFF and embellishments are typically either in a JPEG or PNG format. Each format has its own set of particulars regarding how they are applied, worked with and saved and we'll address each in more detail later.

Once you begin to work on a digital page, you'll need to go to "Save As" under "File" on the Menu bar and select a location to save the document. My preference is to create a folder called WIP (Work in Progress) and save the digital pages there until they are complete. Each page will need to have a unique name. It is very important that you work with JPEG copies and not the original so that any changes you make on your digital scrapbook page do not alter your original. Save your page frequently while you are working on it so as not to lose your hard work by accident.

Other selections that will be made from the Menu bar may include the preset manager and fill layer under "Edit" as well as resize under "Enhance". As you become more comfortable with the basics of digital scrapbooking, there are numerous other selections to take advantage of, but for the purposes of this initial introduction, a minimum number of choices are described.

PHOTOSHOP® ELEMENTS TOOLS

Digital scrapbooking in *Adobe Photoshop® Elements* involves more than just moving photos, documents and embellishments onto a background or other layer. The tools that appear on the left side of the desktop enable a number of other alterations and enhancements to be made to the page.

At the bottom of the desktop, next to the Photo Bin icon, there is another icon listed as "Tool Options". You'll notice that when "Tool Options" is selected and you click on any tool, the Tool Option panel provides a number of choices specific to that particular tool. The question mark in the upper right corner of the Tool Options bin takes you to an *Adobe* tutorial on the uses of the tool that you have selected.

Below is a brief review of the tools frequently used in the process of digital scrapbooking.

Figure 7. Example of the Tool Bar

The uppermost View group includes a Magnifying Glass icon and a Hand icon. The Magnifying Glass allows you to zoom in and out to have a better view of an area on your page. The Hand icon helps to select the size of the item on your desktop.

In the Select group, the tool that is located in the upper left is the Move Tool. This is used frequently to move items from the Photo Bin onto the desktop and to resize or reposition items on a page.

The Red Eye Removal tool in the Enhance group is a handy tool for altering photos that require this type of correction.

Another frequently used tool is the Type tool located in the lower left of the Draw group. Numerous fonts are available and provide the opportunity to type on any section of your page. The color of the type as well as the style, size and direction are some of the many options that there are to work with when using this tool.

In the Modify group, the tool in the upper left corner is the Crop tool. This tool allows you to change the amount of a document that is included in the page or to cut away sections of a photo that are not important.

Finally, at the bottom of the Tool Bar is the Color Picker. Its default shows a black foreground color and a white background color. A color in any photo can be perfectly matched by clicking on the Color Picker tool. Then, using the eye-dropper, click on the spot where you wish to copy a color.

PHOTOSHOP® ELEMENTS LAYER PANEL

When using the traditional method of scrapbooking, it is customary to begin with a sheet of paper as the background, and then add to it in layers. For instance, one might select a black cardstock background, add a patterned paper swatch, a photo, a frame around the photo, a journaling tag, some embellishments and a title block with letter stickers.

Digital scrapbooking utilizes the same concept of adding one layer on top of another to create a page. To work in layers, you'll be using the Layer grid in the Layer Panel to the right of the desktop.

Each time a photo or other document, embellishment or other item is moved from the Photo Bin at the bottom of the desktop into the center of the desktop, a new layer will be created in the Layer Panel. Each layer has an eye icon to the left of it. By clicking on the eye, the layer visibility can be changed from visible to invisible for that specific layer. This can be very helpful when trying to determine if you like the look of a page with or without an item.

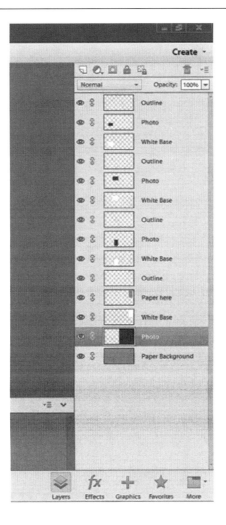

Figure 8. Example of the Layer Panel

By right-clicking on the layer, the option of renaming the layer appears. This is very useful, especially when a page can contain multiple items. Items are easier to locate when they have a unique name rather   than Layer 1, Layer 2 which is automatically assigned to a new layer by default. Layers can be moved up and down in the stack by clicking and holding on them while you drag them to relocate them to another spot in the Layer Panel. This is similar to moving a piece of paper in the stack that you might have on a physical desktop when using traditional scrapbooking.

The opacity (lack of transparency) of the layer can be changed by using the slide bar at the top right hand side of the Layer Panel. Just slide the bar to the right or left depending on the look you're trying to achieve.

A layer can be deleted by right-clicking on it and then selecting "delete" or by holding down and moving to the trash bin at the top right of the Layer Panel.

TEMPLATES

Along with the photo editing software, templates are an invaluable tool when it comes to digital scrapbooking. By using a template, there is no need to create the basic design of the digital scrapbook page. There are numerous template designs available for purchase on the Internet. They are inexpensive and well worth the investment, especially when you consider the time-saving and creative design factors that they offer.

I prefer the templates sold by *YinDesigns* out of Singapore. Not only does this designer offer a wide range of selections, which she is continually adding to, but her template designs lend themselves to very creative works of art and are simple to use, embellish and alter. Unlike others that I've found, hers are very conducive to genealogy scrapbook pages because there are so many areas to include photos, documents and other items. Her templates can be purchased from yindesigns.blog-spot.com then downloaded for multiple use. The purchase price is typically around $1.25 per template or $2.50 per set of two templates each template with 2 – 12" by 12" pages. There are occasional specials that are offered and if you sign up for her newsletter, you'll receive a notification of these offers. By watching my blog, BarbwireDigi.com, you'll see that occasionally discounts are offered on templates and other useful scrapbooking tools.

The template will be either one 12" x 12" page or a two page spread each being 12" x 12". If you have a lot of information, you'll want to use the two page spread. If not, then a one page template will suffice. However, if you are putting your pages into a book, you'll want to be mindful of what you'll see when open to a two page layout.

After I purchase a set of templates and download them to my computer, I file each in a folder in my computer's scrapbooking library and name it

as the number associated with the templates, i.e. Yin template 35 and
36.

Figure 9. File Folders containing Templates

Templates will be in a PSD format which is not able to be viewed outside
of the Adobe Photoshop® software. For that reason, it is wise to also
save a JPEG image of the template along with the template (PSD) in the
same file folder. Frequently, a sample scrapbook page using a particular
template will be supplied by the site where you purchase the template.
These sample pages show how the template has been used to design a
scrapbook page and can make it easier to choose which template you'd
like to use for the creation of your own page. Here is an example of the
file folder containing the PSD template, a JPEG of the template image
and sample scrapbook pages for two templates.

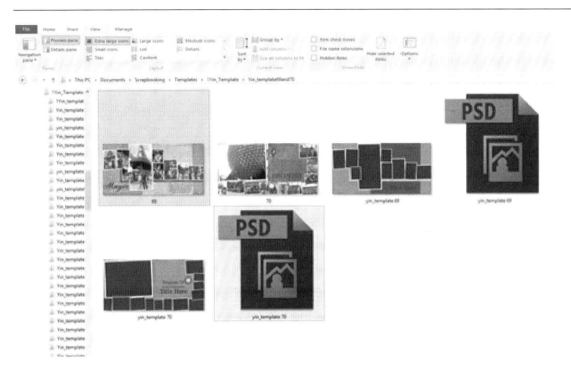

Figure 10. Items within a Template File Folder

Each download will also include the TOU (terms of use) and some informational pages on alternations in formatting so they can be made into a commercially printed scrapbook. According to the terms of use, these templates may be used in part or in whole for private use. I save one set of these in the Yin Design Template master folder.

STEP BY STEP PROCESS

Now that you know the equipment and tools that you need and have a basic understanding of the software and the templates, let's go through a detailed step by step process of creating a digital genealogy scrapbook page. "Print Screen" photos have been included to help clarify each of the steps.

The page we will be creating includes all of the following basic steps:

1. Plan what you'd like to include on the page and get ideas for the general design of the page from other sources,

2. Select an appropriate template that best matches the design of a page you like,

3. Open Adobe Photoshop® Elements – Editor and then select the Expert option,

4. In the Adobe Photoshop Elements software: Open the template, your photos, and other documents which will be included in the page,

5. Be sure to save the template under a new name into the WIP (work in progress) file folder,

6. Add your photos and documents to the template,

7. Add background paper(s),

8. Add journaling, labels, stories, interviews, etc. to the page,

9. Create a Title, Table of Contents, Sections and/or Source or Index page if so desired,

10. Embellish the page with PNG elements, Word Art, etc.,

11. Enhance or alter the page by using brushes, shadows, adjusting transparency, adding color to frames, use blending techniques, etc.,

12. Save the work in a PSD file format, as well as a JPEG format and in a reduced size for the Web,

13. Add video, as well as links to your blog or web page information, if desired,

14. Share with family and friends via print, slide show, blog, email, web, etc., and

15. Print individual pages and place into Family Heirloom Album or order a commercially printed album.

STEP ONE:

PLAN WHAT YOU'D LIKE TO INCLUDE ON THE PAGE AND GET IDEAS FOR THE GENERAL DESIGN OF THE PAGE FROM OTHER SOURCES.

Begin by thinking about the overall look and feel of your family photo album. You may choose to have it include either one family line or multiple lines, one ancestor or multiple ancestors; you might work forward from the earliest ancestor you have on record or work backwards from you or your children. Be sure to think about your audience as well as the records, photos, stories and documents that you have on hand. You may choose to include a Table of Contents, Sections, a Source page and/or to color code various parts of you album. It's best to make some of these decisions before you start the album so you can be consistent throughout.

For the purpose of my Digital Genealogy Scrapbook Album example, I chose four generations on my father's side – The Schwermans – beginning with my great-grandfather, and including my grandfather, father and sibling. For each generation, I'm including information about their spouses, their children and the times they lived in, stories I've heard or know about them as well as photos and supporting documents.

As you begin work on each Digital Genealogy Scrapbook page in the album, you should have a general idea as to what you know of this ancestor, or family, what you want the page to say and what visual materials you have or will want to use in order to present the facts. Remember, it's helpful to place all of your documents that you might want to use in a folder on your desktop. This will make it easier to access what is needed for the page once you begin the process.

I chose to make this two page layout about my Grandfather, Fred Schwerman, and his wife, Ruth (Bauer) for the purpose of this demonstration. I have photos of them as a young couple as well a love note from my grandmother to my grandfather that I want to use. I also want to include his birth certificate and their marriage certificate.

The designs that I found on the website http://www.designerdigitals.com that gave me some inspiration for the page are shown below. I like how one design inserted the documentation off to the side and how the other utilized blending and a look of transparency.

Figure 11. MJRooney – "My Hero" [3]

Figure 12. JustbnSharon – "Legacy"[4]

STEP TWO:

SELECT AN APPROPRIATE TEMPLATE THAT BEST MATCHES THE DESIGN OF A PAGE YOU LIKE.

Now that you have your plan in mind, purchase / select the template by using some of the design ideas from pages you like as a guide. You'll also want to consider what you want the page to reveal and how many documents, photos and other items you have to put on the page. This will help you to select the most appropriate template. Keep in mind that the templates are just a starting point and can be altered as you "build" your scrapbook page. The template is set up such that you will be inserting your unique items into the available spots that are shown as frames. Keep in mind these frames can be adjusted in size and location but this is a great starting point. As you develop expertise in scrap booking, you'll find that you may not always use a template or that you begin with one and alter it as needed while developing what your page will look like. No matter what, they make the process quick and easy and in some cases won't require any alteration at all.

So the template that I choose, based on the design I'm trying to create and the documents that I have was be YinDesign Template 358D which looked like this:

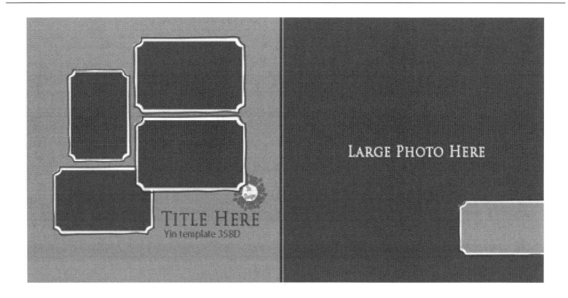

Figure 13. Original YinDesign Template 358D

I then altered it to remove one of the frames on the left side page and to reposition each of the locations for photos and documents in order to better match the design I have in mind. I renamed it Yin-Design Template 358X and here is what the altered template looked like:

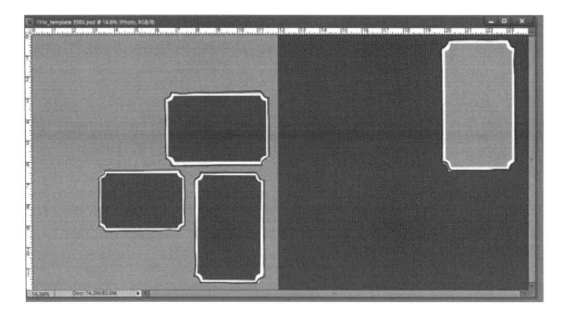

Figure 14. Altered YinDesign Template

You also need to be cognizant of "dead space" if you are planning on printing the page in a commercial photo album. About 1/4" around the page may be deleted by the printer. So do not include anything of importance in this area. In another step, we'll discuss what to do to avoid problems when sending your page off to be put into a commercially produced photo book.

STEP THREE:

OPEN ADOBE PHOTOSHOP® ELEMENTS – EDITOR AND SELECT EXPERT OPTION.

Adobe offers a free trial of its products so you can see if you like it before you make the purchase. Once you have downloaded the photo editing software, you will open it on your computer and it should appear as something like this:

Figure 15. Photoshop Elements Welcome Screen

Then click on "Photo Editor" on the upper right hand side of the
Welcome screen. Once this is done the desktop will appear and you will
see this:

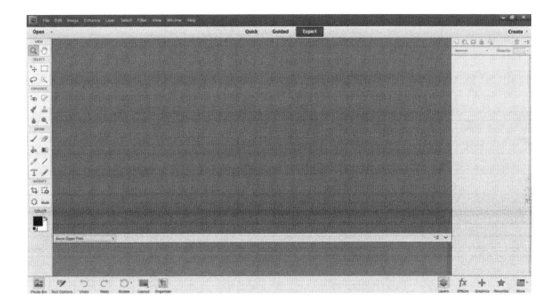

Figure 16. Expert Option in Photoshop Elements

Be sure to select the "EXPERT" option at the top of the screen (right
under the menu bar) by clicking on it.

STEP FOUR:

IN THE ADOBE PHOTOSHOP® ELEMENTS SOFTWARE: OPEN THE
TEMPLATE, YOUR PHOTOS, AND OTHER DOCUMENTS WHICH WILL BE
INCLUDED IN THE PAGE.

First we'll bring the template we've selected into the Adobe Photoshop®
Elements software by doing the following:

• Click on OPEN (upper left just under menu bar),

• Select the location on your computer that contains the template
you've selected and be sure to select the PSD format.

Figure 17. Template in PSD format

• Once you've located the template PSD, selected it and clicked on the "Open" square, it will be loaded into Photoshop elements. You'll notice few changes to your desktop (as shown here). The template will appear in the photo bin (lower left) and there will be several layers in the Layers Panel – such as Background, Title, Photo, Mat, Journaling, etc. (Note: You may see a warning that some fonts are missing. These are merely placeholders and will be replaced or deleted later so no need to be overly concerned about the warning.)

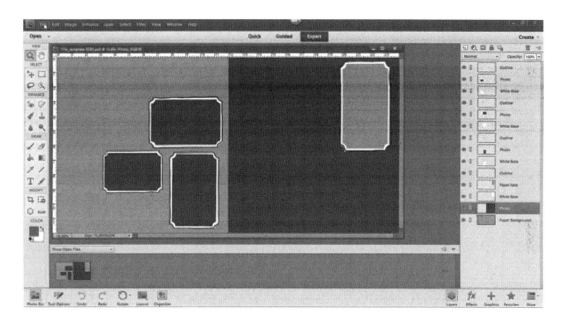

Figure 18. Appearance of Desktop with Template and Layers Panel

• Next we'll bring into the photo editing software any photos that are relative to what our page is telling the viewer. This may include portrait photos, family photos, life events or locations. If the page you are creating is prior to the time of photography or you simply don't have any photographs of this particular ancestor, you may consider other options such as, a photograph of a map of the area they originated from, a photo of the city at the time, a photo the location or home, a photo relating to one of their interests, grave site photos; anything for that matter that helps you tell the story.

Scan any photos that you may have collected and file them on your computer. My recommendation is to use a system such as the one described by Nancy Loe, in her *Guide to Cataloging Digital Family Photographs and Records.* You can order it at *http://www.sassyjanegenealogy.com/guides/cataloging-digital-family-photographs/*. As mentioned previously, it's important that you have an organized system. So, when it comes time to make your digital scrap book, you can easily find the items that you want to use.

• You'll also want to include some of the documents you've gathered that support the knowledge you've gained about the ancestor. This may include the census showing their family and location, naturalization registration, military draft registration, newspaper articles, church records, etc. Scan these documents into your computer, formatting them as a JPEG. Don't worry about the size of the document, because there are tools in Adobe Photoshop® Elements to crop, reduce, highlight or otherwise alter the image to fit in the area that we have to work with. I should mention, this is one of the reasons you may choose to use the 12" x 12" inch size for your album. It will make it easier to include some of your documents and make them easier to read in the finished product.

The steps in this part of the process, bringing photographs and documents in the Adobe Photoshop® Elements program, is exactly like what was used to bring the template onto the desktop. First click on "OPEN" – just beneath the menu bar on the upper left. Then find the file with the photo(s) and other document(s) that you are going to use on the digital scrapbook page. You should hold down the control key while selecting each item if they are not arranged consecutively in the file folder. Then select the "open" command which will bring them into the Photo Bin on the desktop. You'll see that they are all stacked on top of one another. Not to worry, just double-click on the template in the Photo Bin (which should be the furthest to the left) and it will automatically bring your template back up to the desktop (see figure 19).

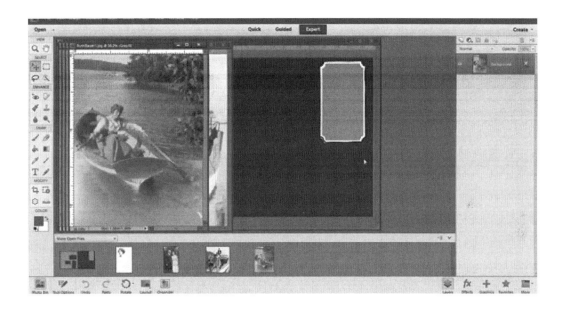

Figure 19. Photos and Documents appear on the Desktop and in the Photo Bin

You don't necessarily have to bring everything into the Adobe Photoshop® Elements desktop that you have initially, nor do you have to use everything that you have opened to the desktop. Either can be added or deleted at a later time.

STEP FIVE:

"SAVE AS" AND THEN "SAVE" PERIODICALLY DURING THE PROCESS OF CREATING YOUR DIGITAL SCRAPBOOK PAGE.

You'll then want to choose "SAVE AS" under "File" in the menu bar and pick a new name and location in which to save the scrapbook page that you are working on. If you neglect to do this, you will be altering your template page. Obviously you don't want to permanently alter the template page, since it can be used to create multiple different designs.

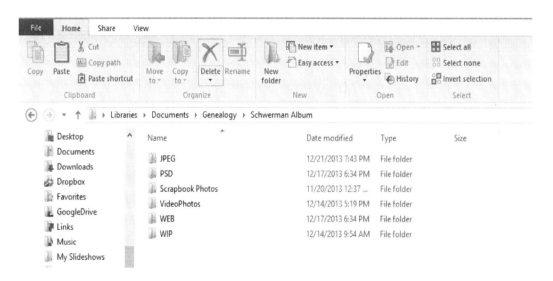

Figure 20. Files for Saving Various Formats of each Page

I suggest naming a folder with the family name such as in this case – "Schwerman Album". Then, in this file folder create another folder entitled "WIP" (work in progress), another which is named "PSD", and another that is named "JPEG and finally, one that is named "Web".

More on these to follow. However, start by saving this page with the template, photos and documents that you've just opened into the WIP folder and naming it Page One (1). The order that the pages are put in the book can always be changed but it's nice to start with some semblance of order in the file folder.

This system will also help you to be able to quickly locate the file folder where all your scrapbook pages can be found as well as individual pages that you are working on or have finished.

Did I mention before how really important it is to save your work? Sooner or later, you'll learn the hard way if you neglect this important aspect of digital scrapbooking. It is also very important to save your page in the PSD file format, if you want to maintain all the layers of your page. This is especially important if you ever want to come back to a page to change a name,

STEP SIX:

ADD THE SELECTED PHOTOGRAPHS AND DOCUMENTS TO THE TEMPLATE.

Now comes what I consider to be the fun part of creating your digital scrapbook page. It's when you'll also see why it's so nice to use a designer's template.

The very first and most important thing to do, if you haven't already, is to click "File" on the menu bar and go to "Save As". You'll want to rename your template to the name of your page. If you neglect to do this your template will be altered, making it difficult to reuse again as a new template. Save your page to a "Work in Progress" Folder and name it something like your ancestor's surname and page 1, or whatever will help you to differentiate one page from another as you create each of them. Note the order of the pages can still be altered and is not fixed. Just because you've put a page number in the title doesn't mean it will have to be located as such in your album.

On the desktop, you will need to have the Photo Bin selected in the task bar at the bottom and select the Move Tool from the tool bar on the left of the desktop. Double click on the template that appears in the Photo Bin so that when you look at the desktop, it is what you see in the center. You'll also see all the layers of the template listed to the right in the Layer Panel.

Next, select any one of the black areas within the template in which you wish to put a photo or document, by clicking on it. You'll notice that the layer is highlighted in the layers panel, matching the area on the template that you've selected.

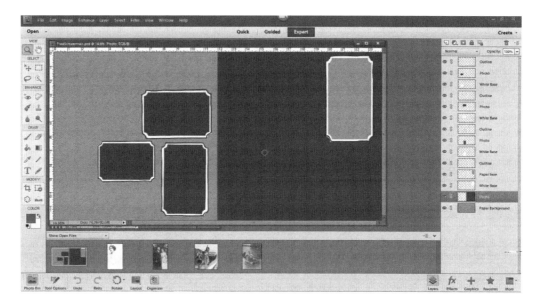

Figure 21. Select an area in the template in which to place
a photo or a document

Then select an item from the photo bin, by clicking on it, and while
holding on the item while dragging it up into the template on the desktop. It will sometimes appear in the center of the desktop and need to be
moved to the preferred location using the Move Tool. It will likely need
to be resized as well. You'll notice that in the Layer Panel a new layer is
created immediately above the layer that is named "Photo".

To resize, use the Move Tool from the tool bar and click on one of the
corner markers located on each side and center of the photo, then drag
to either enlarge or shrink the photograph. It helps to hold the shift key
while adjusting the corners, so that the proportions remain the same
and your photograph does not become distorted. When you want to tilt
the photo to more closely align with the box it's going to be put in, just
hover with the mouse on the corner square. When an arrow appears,
hold on it and shift from the right or the left depending on how you'd
like to tilt the photograph. If you don't like how it looks, click the red "x".
If you do like the outcome, click the green check mark to lock it in. You

can always use the undo selection in the task bar to make changes.

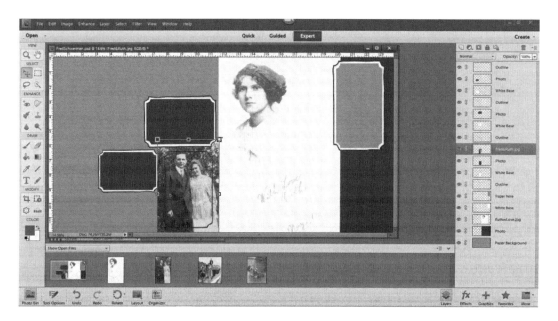

Figure 22. Resize by using the Move Tool on the corner markers

You may notice that the photo does not fit exactly into the frame. Don't worry. It's easy to get the exact portion of the photo into the frame without having to struggle to make it fit just right by using the Move Tool. If you look to the Layer Panel, you'll see that the layer is highlighted with the photo that you've just moved. It may be named as well with the name you have it filed under in your document folder. If not, you can always name it by right-clicking on the layer and then selecting "rename "layer. This is very helpful when you have a lot of layers and may wish to reposition them later on. You'll see there is a layer below your photo in the Layer Panel that says "photo". If you hover the mouse between these two layers while holding down the "ALT" key, the hand icon will change to a small black and white box. When it appears, click on it. If your photo was larger than the frame, you will now see only the portions that appear within the frame on the template. You can still click on the photo on the desktop template to move it within the frame or to resize it as before, if you don't care for how it is positioned. If it is too small in the frame, you will need to make it larger by holding on the corner square and shift key and dragging diagonally. It's important to select either the red x or green check after you're done or you won't be able to move on.

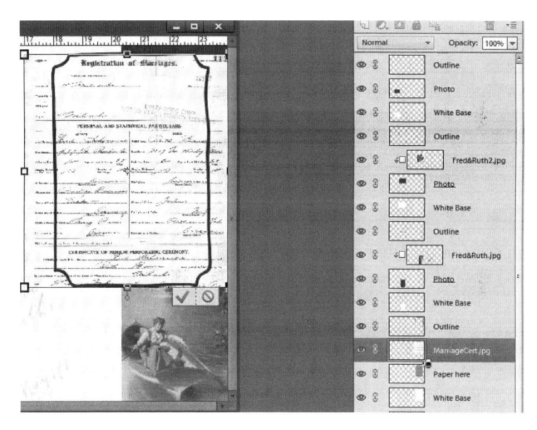

Figure 23. While hovering between layers, hold the "ALT" key and then click to commit to the frame.

If you don't see the photo in the frame, then it means that you have your photo above the wrong layer in the Layer Panel. You may have neglected the first step of selecting the frame before dragging the photo to the desktop. Not to worry. You can easily reposition where the photo is in the Layer Panel by clicking on it and holding while you drag it up or down in the Layer Panel. The small icons on each layer to the left of the name give you some idea of where you are on the template. Another way to tell which layer you want or where you're currently at in comparison, is to click on the "Eye icon" that appears on the left side of each layer. This changes the visibility of the layer. When you click on the eye, it turns the layer off. Clicking it again will turn it back on.

Once you have the photo positioned exactly as you'd like it on the page, be sure to go to the Menu bar, select file and then "Save". Then continue to do the same thing with all the photos and documents that you have placed in the Photo Bin. Save the PSD document after each addition, so you will not risk losing your work.

STEP SEVEN:

ADD BACKGROUND PAPER(S).

Unlike traditional scrapbooking, where the page creator typically will begin with the background page, pile each additional piece on top of it and then secure it to the background and/or other layers with adhesive, my preference is to apply the background toward the end. I do this because I like to incorporate or contrast the colors in the photos and other items with the background paper(s) that I use.

The background layer or layers appear at the bottom of the Layer Panel (two background layers will appear if you're using a two page template). Papers that are used for the background can be purchased in kits or separately. Or they can be created by taking a digital photograph of a paper you already have or by scanning a document and then saving it as a digital document.

Putting a paper into your background is accomplished by using a method similar to what was used when adding photos and documents to a page. You'll select the layer that appears at the bottom of the Layer Panel, entitled "Paper Background". Then, as before, click on "Open" on the desktop under the menu bar and select the JPEG of the paper you have chosen to use from the files on your computer. If you want more than one paper on the page, you can add an additional layer and bring in a second, or a third paper. Use the Move Tool to adjust the position of the paper(s) to your liking.

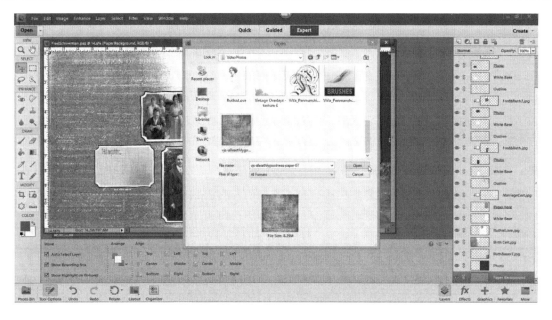

Figure 24. Open Background paper for placement on the page.

You can see on the above example that a JPEG of a purchased paper (vjs – All Earthy Goodness.) was used on the right-hand side page and the document showing the Registration of Birth was used as the background paper on the left-hand side page.

Other, more advanced, techniques afford you the opportunity to adjust the transparency of the papers on the page, to blend pages together, to add designs with brushes – all of which add to the creative, art-like look of the page. Many of the tutorials, that were mentioned previously, assist you in learning more about these additional creative touches.

Remember, you can always use "Undo" in the Task Bar as you are creating the page, if you decide you don't like the looks of something. A new layer should be created (and named) for each set of changes or new addition you are making to your page so, if you don't care for it, you can easily delete that layer from the Layer Panel. But also remember that it's equally important that you "Save", so if and when you do like what's on the page you won't lose it.

STEP EIGHT:

ADD JOURNALING, LABELS, STORIES, INTERVIEWS, ETC. TO THE PAGE.

Of course, the whole point of making a digital genealogy scrapbook is to share more than just the photos and the documents you've uncovered. You want to tell the whole story of what you've learned about your family. Nothing is more frustrating than looking at an old photo album and wondering who the people are in the picture. And who wants to look a family photo that merely states "right to left" ... "Mary Miller, Joseph Bauer, Ruth ... " like a high school yearbook?

So the journaling on your page will be the most important part. It not only ties together what you've found but it relays to others more than they can gather from the items you've placed on the page. Take a second look at your page after the photos and documents are in it and ask yourself – if my children's children's children look at this page decades from now will they know the who, what, where and when that I want to share about this individual and their life as I know it? Will they know the stories that make us uniquely who we are? Or will they just see a bunch of photos with a name and a date and a census page with facts and figures? With that in mind, let's move on to the next, most important step.

Journaling can be accomplished in a number of ways –

You can write out or type a piece that "tells the story", scan/save it as a JPEG and then bring it into your page in a similar fashion to what you've done with your photos, by putting it into one of the frames.

You can make it a part of the background – which is like slipping a piece of paper behind the photos and documents and then moving items so you can see all that's been written.

You can use the Text Tool and create a line of text, a text box or boxes and type anywhere you want on the page – even directly onto any photo or document.

You can add a journaling tag as an embellishment and type on it.

You can add a banner, or a "sticker", a date stamp, a caption, or a title that helps give the viewer more information.

Or you can add a video of an interview you've conducted by putting a QR code on the page, linking it to a video you've made and saved to your personal YouTube or Screencast site. More on this useful technique follows in a later step.

Let's go into more detail on the "how to" of some of the journaling methods mentioned above. Both one and two above have been described previously (steps six and seven), so let move on to the third method and discuss the use of the Text Tool.

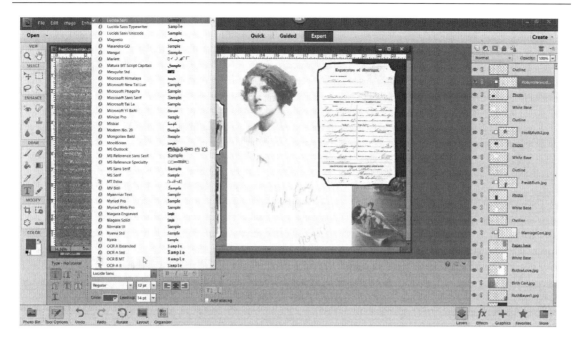

Figure 25. Tool Options task bar provides choices for the Text Tool.

First select the layer in the Layer Panel where you want the text to appear. It will be highlighted as you can see in the above example. Then click on the Text tool in the Tool bar – its icon looks like the letter "T". In the Task bar below the desk top, choose Tool Options (to the right of the Photo Bin). Here you will find a number of choices that can be made about the text that is going to be put on the page. When using the Type Tool to add journaling to the page, select size 12 font, as it is usually the easiest to read. The best font types to use include Myriad Pro or Times New Roman. You can also select the color that you want the font to be, how you'd like it to be aligned, the spacing between lines, as well as whether you'd like it to appear bold or in italics. After you've made these decisions, click on the template, select where you want the type to appear and begin to type a line of text. You can always use the Move Tool to reposition the text exactly where you'd like it to appear.

If you'd need to have more than just a few words or a line of text on the page, then it is best to create a text box. To do so, click on the Text

Tool. Then select on the upper left corner of the space where you'd like to place the journaling block, click and hold as you draw downward down to the lower right-hand side creating a text box. Then, using the task options after picking the Text tool, select the font, size, color, etc. and begin to type the paragraph within the text box.

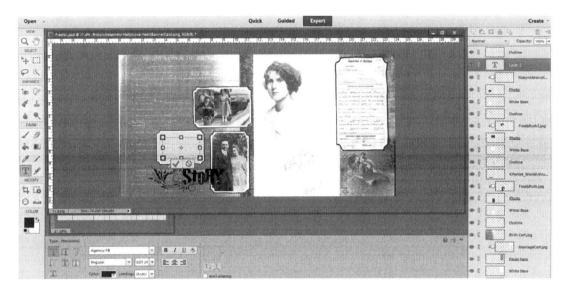

Figure 26. Create a text box to type more than one line of journaling.

You'll learn more in some of the upcoming steps about adding embellishments, tags, using date stamps, etc. but the basic principles apply no matter where you want to include text by using the Text Tool. Individual words or quotes can also add an interesting element to the page and are available as embellishments for purchase or you can create your own using Word Art.

No matter what method you choose, don't neglect this very important step of adding journaling. Using your own handwriting is a valuable addition, even if you never have liked how it looks. It will be a meaningful addition to the album in years to come. Just as including a document such as, a draft registration with your ancestors own signature on it, is a unique and interesting part of any page. Anything personal can help "bring to life" more of who the people were that are now a part of who we are. Adding an interview or other video will be covered in another section of this guide. It's probably the best way to personalize your page or digital genealogy scrapbook album!

STEP NINE:

CREATE A TITLE, TABLE OF CONTENTS, SECTIONS AND/OR SOURCE OR INDEX PAGE, IF SO DESIRED.

TITLE:

After your page contains the photos, documents and journaling, you may wish to include a title. It is not essential but it could be just what's needed to give the viewer more information about the subject of the page.

On the YinDesign templates we're using there is a layer that says "title". Merely select the layer in the Layer Panel that is named "Title" by clicking on it and then select the Text Tool in the tool bar. As before, choose the font style, color, size, etc. that you prefer. You will want to use a font size much larger than the previous size 12 and you will want to make it Bold so that it will stand out.

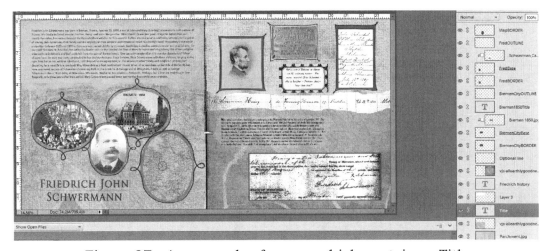

Figure 27. An example of a page which contains a Title

In the example in Figure 27, the name Friedrich John Schwermann was used as the title to the page. Even though the reader would be able to figure out that's who the page is about, it's a nice addition that makes it clear which ancestor the page is giving information about. The title doesn't always have to be the name of an individual. It may be a place, an event, a favorite quote, whatever you feel best describes the general subject of the page. A title is not essential and if you don't wish to add one, then you are by no means obligated to do so.

TABLE OF CONTENTS:

To help guide your viewer through the digital genealogy scrapbook   album you may also consider making the first page a Table of contents. It may be just what's needed to assist in creating some semblance of   order to the flow of your document. This is especially true if you have a number of individuals, families or generations included in your album.

Perhaps the Table of Contents could be as simple as this page shown in Figure 28 which was posted on www.designerdigitals.com named *muddy_bootsweb.jpg* using the "Done with Doilies", by Katie Pertiet. I envision the upper left corner could say "Schwerman Family Album". Then each photo would be of one ancestor and the page number or   section of the album would be typed on the photo or beneath it in order to help the viewer find where in the album their story is contained.

Figure 28. Sample of Potential Design
for a Table of Contents Page [5]

SECTIONS:

If your digital album is going to include more than one individual, or family or generation, you may find that it is beneficial to break up the pages into sections. To do so, it would help to add a Section Title to indicate to the viewer the change for one to the next. Each section might also contain not only the Title but also a photo of the Family tree or Family Group page. Color coding the sections by using a similar color on the background page is also a possibility. This could include Section titles with a document outlining what is covered in that particular section. Or photo groupings that indicate individuals or events included in each family sections. The possibilities are limitless.

SOURCES:

For those who want to show that their research is documented a final page or pages can provide a listing of the sources used on each of the documents in the album, page by page. To clarify even further, a number or letter or other indicator could be typed on the corner of a document and then referenced on a page at the back of the album. A Link could also be generated to indicate where to find a document with the sources that are included in the album as well as other information that the interested individual could refer to even if it was not included in the album but was used in the research.

STEP TEN:

EMBELLISH THE PAGE WITH PNG ELEMENTS, WORD ART, ETC.

Up until now you may be thinking, I could do virtually all of this by using any of the commercial programs that are available through several companies such as Snapfish, Shutterfly Picaboo, etc. But one of the major differences with the programs associated with the commercial designs, is that you are not given the latitude to create what works best for your particular needs. You are also limited by the variety of papers and embellishments offered.

Without the use of embellishments, the page might be rather boring – just photos and documents appear as though they were pasted on a background with a colored sheet of paper behind them. So what are embellishments? Simply said, anything that might embellish or add to the beauty and artistic flavor of the page. This can range the gamut from tags to ribbons, stitching, arrows, flowers, diagrams, words, vintage articles, buttons, paper clips, staples and more. There are various forms of embellishments, some are found as JPEG files and others are PNG files. Embellishments are available to purchase and be downloaded from a number of different scrapbooking sites and are almost always included when you order a kit of any sort. You can also create your own by taking a photo of a memento or scanning an item to put it into a digital format.

Remember, the object of creating a digital genealogy scrapbook page is to catch the attention of the viewer. More importantly, you want to hold their attention such that they will want to look at the display of the information you've uncovered about the family. One of the best ways to do so is to add embellishments that help to create an artistic look to the page. So then, let's review just how we go about adding various embellishments to our page.

Figure 29. Layer is highlighted when selected in the Layer Panel.

Select the layer in the Layer Panel that closely matches approximately where on the page you would like the embellishment to go. Above the Layer Panel, to the left side there is an Icon that when selected will "Create a new Layer". Or, you can go to the menu bar and under Layer, select "new" and then pick "layer". As before, click on "Open" under the menu bar and select the embellishments that you have purchased and saved to the file folder on your computer. The embellishment you select may appear in the center of the page. If so, click on the Move Tool and use it to reposition the embellishment to where you want it on the page. If you don't see it at all, chances are that the layer is too low in the Layer Panel. Merely click on the highlighted layer which should be the embellishment and hold it while you drag the layer upward in the Layer

Panel until the embellishment appears on the desktop. Then release the layer. If the embellishment is a PNG, it is on a transparent layer, so in order to reposition it you will need to click on any visible part of the image. If necessary, zoom in by using the Magnifying Glass in the tools in order to see the image. Create a new layer before adding each embellishment. Save your work when you have finished adding each.

STEP ELEVEN:

ENHANCE OR ALTER THE PAGE BY USING BRUSHES, SHADOWS, ADJUSTING TRANSPARENCY, USING MASKS OR OVERLAYS, ADDING COLOR TO FRAMES, ETC.

At this point, the page is almost complete. You may choose to stop here and consider it finished or make some additional enhancements or alterations to the page.

For example, the frames on the template surrounding the photo are generally all the same and rather boring. Color can easily be added to the border to help make the photo stand out or blend into the page. Just select the "mat" layer in the layers panel, choose the Color Picker tool at the bottom of the tool bar and use the eye-dropper to sample the color from the photo or go with a standard color. Then use the Paint Bucket from the tool bar to apply the color to the mat which you have selected. Don't worry if you don't like it, you can always select "Undo".

Figure 30. Adding color to a frame as an enhancement.

You might also decide to change the shape of the photo and mat or the size of a grouping or the placement on the page. Just select the mat, clipping mask and photo (by clicking on one, holding the shift key and then clicking on the remaining two layers), then use the Move Tool and either reshape, resize or change the location of the photo/document and mat on the page.

Drop shadows can be added to any of the objects on the page by selecting any layer and then choosing Effects in the task panel. Styles such as a beveled look or gradient can also be used to alter images on the page.

When a layer is selected in the layers panel, you'll notice that a slider bar appears at the top right of the Layer Panel which allows you to change the transparency of the layer. This can help create a subtle look to whatever item has been selected.

Other tools can add some real interest to the page. Brushes can be loaded to add scrolls, lines, clusters of color, watercolor effects and much more. Masks can also be added to the page to provide a vintage look or a darkened effect along the edges of the page or to block from view select areas. Overlays can be added to create a darkened or shadowed area around the edges or along various parts of the page.

A popular alteration is called blending. This alteration can be used to blend a photo into a background paper, blend two or more papers together or to create a softened look to an otherwise stark photo. Here is an example of blending that was used to create an interesting effect on a photo that was originally a stark black and white image. Blending helps to create a more of an artistic feel and softens the page.

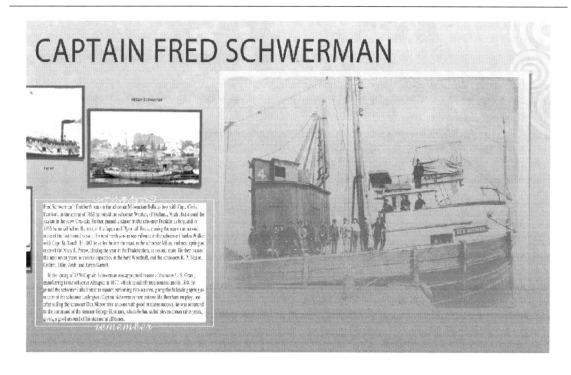

Figure 31. An example of the Blending Technique used on a Page.

Figure 32. The stark Black and White photo prior to Blending.

There are numerous tutorials available to assist you in these and many other alterations. Do as much as you like or as little to generate the look you're after for your page.

STEP TWLEVE:

SAVE THE WORK IN A PSD FILE FORMAT, AS WELL AS JPEG FORMAT AND IN A REDUCED SIZE FOR THE WEB.

Throughout the process of creating your digital scrapbook pages, it is extremely important to SAVE your results. As mentioned in the section on templates, begin by renaming and saving your template to WIP.

Once the page is complete you'll want to save it to three locations. First, save it as a PSD (Photoshop) page in the file labeled PSD. This is important in case you'd ever like to do any future editing of the page, making additions, corrections or any other alterations or changes. This is the only way to preserve all the layers that make up the digital page.

Then go to Save as, change the file type to JPEG, and save your creation to the file folder labeled JPEG. This file folder is where you will store all of the final pages for use in making an album. As JPEG files they are ready to be printed to insert into a binder, uploaded to be published in a commercial photo album, imported into PowerPoint to be used as a slide show or printed individually to be framed and displayed.

Finally, the page should be saved in a smaller scale for more efficient use on the web. To do so, under File in the menu bar, select "Save for the web". On the right side you'll need to change the size to 600 pixels. And select JPEG. Then save in the file folder named WEB. These pages can then be shared on a blog, via email, on the web or on social media.

Note that the pages saved as JPEG and for the WEB will be flattened images and no longer will show each of the individual layers, making it virtually impossible to alter the page. This is why it is so important to always save a PSD file format of every page you create.

Chapter Four: Example of the Process

To view a video of the process of creating the two pages which are
illustrated below – paste this link into your browser:
http://www.screencast.com/t/8Nb9B5dbtVF or visit YouTube and
search for the video there.

Figure 33. The two page spread demonstrated in the video.

Chapter Five: Adding Video

With the advances in technology it is possible to make your scrapbook "come alive". Let's say you've had the chance to interview a relative to find out what they remember about ancestors that you may never have had the opportunity to meet. Or perhaps you have a video that could really add to a page you're creating by telling your story using visual and audio effects. The process isn't difficult and it can make a great addition to your scrapbook page and album. Here's how:

Begin by creating your scrapbook page as usual but leave a small space for a small square box that will contain a QR Code. Virtually everyone has been exposed to QR Codes (Quick Response Codes) which appear on retail products, magazine pages, and numerous other places in our day to day lives. They are those unusual looking square barcodes that can be scanned with an electronic device like a smartphone that has a bar-code-reader app. Once you do so, you're taken to a link with more information, a coupon or in this case, a YouTube video.

Next, create the video using whatever means you prefer. Save it to your computer as a MPV. Then upload to the website of your choosing such as YouTube or Screencast. If you are concerned about privacy just be sure that your settings are set to "Private" so that only those with the link or QR code can view them. Or you can look into hosting your videos on your blog or in other places. You'll need to note and copy the unique URL link that is associated with the video you've recorded and uploaded.

Then you need to create a QR code. There are several sites, both free and for a fee, that provide you the opportunity to create a QR code for your use. Two such sites are *Kaywa*™ or *BeQRious*. If you print your pages using Picaboo®, you can create the QR code right on their site. Once your QR code is generated, right click on the QR code image and select "copy image" to copy it to your computer's clipboard. Or in the case of *Picaboo®*, just add it to a page in your scrapbook. Each QR code you generate can then be linked to the video of your choice using the URL (http://....).

Finally, in your photo editing software with your page open, create a new layer in the Layers panel on the page that you'd like to include the video in. Then paste the QR code onto your page and place it where you want it to be by using the move tool to position it where you'd like it to be. You may wish to add the words: "watch this video", "meet Grandma" or "see the full story" - next to the QR code. When using *Picaboo®*, just add it to the finished page. Try to incorporate the code into the design of your page so it doesn't stand out but rather blends into the look of the page.

Save the page in a JPEG format. However, be sure to save your page in a PSD format with the layers as well, so that when QR codes are obsolete, you can eliminate the useless QR code from your page are replace with any new technology.

Then test the QR code embedded on the digital scrapbook page. To do so just complete the following steps:

1) Open up a barcode reader app on your smartphone or other electronic device,

2) Scan the QR code using the device's camera (you can scan from the printed page or directly from the computer screen),

3) Once the app recognizes the QR code you'll be taken to the additional

content and

4) Then view the video.

You'll want to be sure that it works prior to saving or printing the page for your album. As a side note, you don't have to use QR codes for links to just videos. Consider generating QR codes for blog posts with additional photos related to your page or sources of the research. You could even link to information about a historical site or to anything else on the web for that matter.

Chapter Six: Edits and Changes

Once you've completed the first draft of your album, you'll need to go back through each of the pages and make a double check that all is just the way you want it. Be sure to conduct a spell-check on each of the journaling areas. Look over dates and other data to be sure it is as accurate as possible. As long as you've saved your information in a PSD format you'll be able to revise and correct anything that you may need to at a future date. It might be helpful to print out a "trial" version of the album so you can be certain all is perfect before posting or printing the final version.

Another edit you may wish to make is to resize the completed template pages. In particular, if the pages you've created are a two page spread measuring 12" x 24" you'll want to crop the page to 12" by 12". Then save the left hand side with the page # and the letter "A" in the name and save the right hand side as the page # with the letter "B" in the name. This will enable you to have the individual pages printed or up-loaded.

Sources of data can be continually updated as your research progresses. If you've added a QR code with a link to your source document, just be sure it is the latest version before going to press.

A dedication page is a nice added touch. You might also consider including an "About the Author" page or caption. Hopefully your album will stand the test of time and future generations will be interested to know more who you are.

Last but not least, you'll need to create a cover page for both the front and the back of the album. The front might be as simple as the family tree, a family group sheet, or a compilation about the album contents such as the one shown here:

Figure 34. Example of a Cover Page.

The back cover page could be your dedication page, a brief statement of who you are or perhaps why you created this album. For Example:

This is dedicated to those who endured the struggles, delighted in the daily challenges, celebrated the successes of life and made our presents and futures possible. To my Family.

Chapter Seven: Final Version

Once your final version has been perfected and everything is exactly as you want it, you have several options available to you of how to share your work of art with family and friends.

PSD FORMAT:

As I've mentioned on several occasions in this guide, you'll want to save a final version in a file folder label PSD. The documents in this folder should be the original PSD page of each page in the digital scrapbook album. Keep a copy of this saved to a flash drive, the cloud, and external hard drive as well as your computer so you are triple protected in case of the loss of a device. This format allows for future changes to be made to any of the pages if you so desire.

JPEG FORMAT:

Save another version of your digital scrapbook album in the file folder labeled as JPEG. Use a high quality setting. These pages can then be printed and placed in a Heritage Photo Album with page protectors or print and frame any of the pages for display. You might consider printing the pages and putting in albums to give to family members as a birthday or holiday gift.

WEB FORMAT:

Under "File" in the menu bar, there is a "Save for the Web" option. Each page you've created should also be saved for the web and stored in another file folder for this format version. These pages will then be able to be uploaded to your blog, to a social media page, to your web page or other site on the Internet and then shared with others.

POWERPOINT:

Since you album is in a digital format, it is quite easy to use a software program such as Microsoft PowerPoint and create a slideshow presentation to share. This is perfect for a family reunion or even to connect to your television screen during holiday or other special family gatherings, and share with family and friends.

PRINTED ALBUMS:

You may consider uploading the pages to a commercial printing company to have them printed individually or as a commercially-prepared scrapbook album. If you choose the second option, I recommend the lay flat version. Bear in mind that anything on the outer 1/4" of the page may be cut off by the printer, so be sure nothing important runs to the edge of the page. I use *Picaboo®* and then upload each 12" x 12" page as a background page option for each of the pages in the book.

No matter which of the above methods you may choose to use, the most important thing is that you share your hard work. After all your efforts, don't just leave the files on your desktop or other storage device. You've worked hard to display your research in an interesting format so be sure to take the extra time, effort and funds that might be required in order to be sure what you've created is shared and viewed by others.

References

1. http://en.wikipedia.org/wiki/Scrapbooking

2. Jarvik, Elaine (1997-04-23). "Memories & Mementos". Deseret News. p. C1.

3. Design by MJRooney entitled "My Hero" posted on http://www.designerdigitals.com.

4. Design by JustbnSharon entitled "Legacy" posted on. http://www.designerdigitals.com

5. Design posted on www.designerdigitals.com named *muddy_bootsweb.jpg* using the "Done with Doilies", by Katie Pertiet

NOTES:

NOTES:

The WORLD is a BOOK.
Those who do not TRAVEL
read only a page.
St. Augustine

About the Scrapbook Author

I married my high-school sweetheart and we just celebrated our 41st wedding anniversary. I have a son and daughter and two grandchildren. We have our primary residence in Pinedale, Wy. but are both originally from Milwaukee, Wi. We spend time back there so we can enjoy our two grandchildren during the summer months. We reside in Steamboat Springs, Co because we are avid skiers. We also spend a few weeks each year in the Bahamas to soak up the sun and love to cruise whenever we get the chance.

I'm a graduate of University of Wisconsin in Madison and have my masters degree from the Graduate School of Management in Lake Forest, Il. I love to learn and am working at learning Italian and German.

I worked for six years as a dietitian in two Milwaukee area hospitals I then took a sales position with Ross Labs, a division of Abbott Laboratories and worked there for 21 years.

Besides traveling, I love to swim, ski, read, sew, do genealogy research and of course scrapbook! My motto is "Enjoy your life today knowing that no one is promised tomorrow".

20011603R00060

Made in the USA
San Bernardino, CA
23 March 2015